ALASKA BACKYARD WINES

Jan O'Meara

Illustrations by Victoria Hand

Wizard Works
P.O. Box 1125
Homer, Alaska 99603

ACKNOWLEDGEMENTS

To —

Carole Demers, Shirley Forquer, Carolyn Guerra, and Joy Moch, who generously shared their wine recipes,
My husband, Mike, without whose help and encouragement this book would not have been written,
And my good and faithful friends, whose enthusiastic support over the years gave me the idea for the book,

— my heartfelt thanks.

TABLE OF CONTENTS

Introduction 7

1. A Delectable Discovery 9

2. Wine Making Demystified 11

3. A Little of This, a Little of That 15

4. The Words of Wine 17

5. One Step at a Time 23

6. What Can Go Wrong 31

7. From Start to Finish 33

Rapid Reference Section 53

        Steps in Making Wine 55

        Equipment Check List 56

Wine Making Suppliers 58

Other Books on Wine Making 59

Index 61

INTRODUCTION

Wine making is a hobby that produces marvelous rewards — from the pleasant hours spent in the Alaska sunshine gathering material for the wine, to the pleasant hours sipping the wonderful product of your labor. Aside from your own pleasure, one of the most satisfying things about making wine is serving it to your friends and watching their eyebrows lift in surprise and their eyes light up with the delight of discovery that you are the creator of such fine nectar.

Anyone, with just a little time and effort, can turn a wide variety of fruits, flowers, even vegetables, into homemade wines that please both the eye and the palate. And because you are in control of the ingredients, your wines can be as sweet or dry, light or full-bodied as you like.

Most people come to wine making as an experiment. Whether they continue depends, in part, on their experience that first time. Use the best ingredients, follow the directions, and apply lots of patience, and you can produce a first class wine the first time... and every time.

Strictly speaking, grapes are the only fruit which produce a drink called, simply, "wine." All other wines are specified by name, as in Rose Petal Wine. Grapes do not grow in Alaska, of course, nor do many of the fruits, vegetables and flowers listed in other books about wine making. But many plants suitable to wine making do grow in the far north, and from these the Alaska wine maker can produce home wines that rival any produced anywhere in the world.

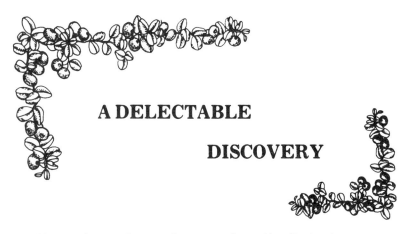

A DELECTABLE DISCOVERY

No one knows how, when, or where the first wine was produced, but by the time people got around to writing about what they do, it was already a popular beverage.

The first batches of wine were probably accidental, the fortuitous result of letting crushed fruit or fruit juice sit around in a warm place for a long time. Most likely, the fruit involved was the grape. Grapes have a natural yeast on their skins and lots of sugar inside; they need little else to turn them into wine. And grapes were being cultivated as early as 6,000 B.C., historians say.

Wine's rapid rise in popularity is understandable. It tasted good; it made the drinker feel good, unless he drank too much; and as settlements poured their effluents into rivers and streams, it was probably a lot safer to drink than water.

Whatever the case, wine was so important for ancient cultures that gods of wine were created and celebrated at different times throughout the year. For the Greeks it was Bacchus, or Dionysus — who represented not only the intoxicating aspects of wine but its benefits as well, so that he was also honored as a promoter of civilization.

For those early cultures, vine and wine were used almost interchangeably. But people have a lot of ingenuity, and it wasn't long until they'd learned to change other fruits into wine as well. Early Egyptian connoisseurs, it is said, had their choice of five types of wine, including date and palm wine. By the Middle Ages, people were turning almost anything that would grow in their gardens into wine. And that practice has continued, unabated, right up until the present time.

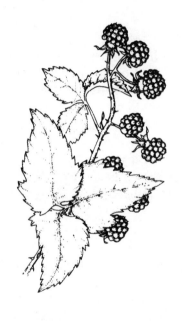

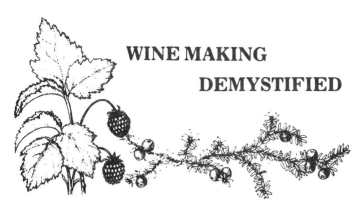

WINE MAKING
DEMYSTIFIED

Wine making is an easy process. Basically, all it requires is some type of plant material, water, sugar, yeast... and lots of patience.

The plant material is necessary to give the wine body and flavor. The water gives it a drinkable consistency. Sugar and yeast work together in a process called fermentation to produce alcohol. And patience is required to let the wine finish.

Almost every type of plant material imaginable — with the possible exception of tree bark and fungi — has been used as a basis for wine. Tree sap, leaves, herbs, flower petals, fruits and berries, grains, vegetables, even vegetable peelings, have gone into the wine maker's vat. The axiom seems to be, use what you have. Of course, some materials make better tasting wine than others. High on the list are fruit, berries, and flowers.

Yeasts are busy little organisms with an almost insatiable appetite for sugar. The by-product they produce is alcohol. Early wine makers probably relied on airborne yeasts or those found on fruit skins. So could we today — any sugary material exposed to the air will eventually ferment — but it is a chancy business. The quality of the wine is chiefly determined by the quality of the yeast, so if you don't know what kind of yeast is going into the wine, you never know what you'll get. And wine left open to attract airborne yeast may also attract the vinegar bacteria — fine if you're trying for vinegar, but not too great for a beverage.

The best yeasts for wine are those that are produced specifically for wine making. Some people say it is all right to use baker's yeast, but typically this leaves a yeasty taste that affects the flavor and bouquet, or aroma, of the wine. The results are always disappointing to anyone hoping to produce a first-rate wine.

There are many types of wine yeast, depending on the region they come from or the type of wine desired. There are yeasts produced especially for champagnes, light white wines and heavier red ones. For most people, though, it may be easiest to start with a simple all-purpose wine yeast and experiment with the others after becoming more experienced wine makers. Although it limits somewhat the type of wine you can make, many outstanding wines can be produced from all-purpose wine yeast. Some of the more specialized yeasts are a little more temperamental, and sometimes more difficult to obtain in Alaska.

For the yeast to work, it needs sugar. Sugar comes in a variety of forms, but the most readily available and easiest to use is plain old granulated white sugar. The yeast likes it and it does not affect the flavor or color of the wine. Brown sugar, used by some home wine makers for color, can overpower the delicate flavor of flower and some fruit wines. Some purists prefer a specialized sugar called dextrose, but it may also be a little harder to find in Alaska.

To a limited extent, the amount of sugar used determines not only how sweet the wine will be, but how strong. It might seem logical that the more sugar there is for the yeast to convert, the higher the alcohol content. But even yeast can get too much of a good thing. Too much sugar at the beginning of the process makes the yeast sluggish and impedes fermentation. Use too much sugar at the start and you are liable to end up with a really sweet wine with a low alcohol content, almost a syrup. The right ratio seems to be between two and three pounds of sugar per gallon of wine.

Yeasts are living organisms. Like you, they have to eat. They need food to keep up their strength and do what they have to do. Generally, they get the nourishment they need from the sugar and the fruit used in making the wine. But sometimes the plant material is low in vitamin content and cannot maintain vigorous yeast action. When this happens, fermentation slows way down or stops altogether.

Fermentation is the crux of the wine making process. Without it, all you have is juice. To keep the process going until a desirable wine has been achieved, many wine makers add yeast nutrient or yeast energizer to each batch of wine. These are, in essence, "vitamins" for the yeast. They keep it healthy and active.

There are other additives that are not necessary to help the yeast work, but help to enhance or protect the flavor of the finished wine. You can make wine without them, but the quality of the finished product is better and more predictable when they have been added.

Grape tannin is a form of tannic acid found in the skin of grapes. Tannic acid adds body to the wine, keeps it from deteriorating, and enhances the flavor. Most fruits contain tannic acid, but not enough to do the job sufficiently.

Some fruits, such as crabapples and cloudberries, contain lots of pectin. This is great for making jams and jellies, but it creates a problem for wine makers. Pectin clouds the wine and leaves a thick residue. To break it down, pectin enzymes are added before fermentation begins.

Perhaps the most controversial additive is potassium or sodium metabisulfite, or Campden tablets. Sulfites are sterilizers. They keep bottles, equipment, even wine, pure and prevent mold or bacteria from developing. They have been used by wine makers, in one way or another, for hundreds of years. However, some people — a rare few — are severely allergic to sulfites and develop alarming reactions. If you use sulfites, and most home wine making experts suggest that you do, it is a good idea to let friends know you do before serving them your homemade wine.

Whatever you put, or don't put, into your wine, there is one thing that is absolutely critical, and that is time. Patience is more than a virtue in wine making; it is a necessity.

Wine making is easy, but it involves a lot of waiting. From gathering fruits or flowers to fermentation may only take a few days, but several months may go by before fermentation stops and the wine is ready to be siphoned into storage jars — a process called racking. Several more months may elapse while the stored wine clears and becomes ready for drinking or final bottling.

This is where many novice wine makers get into trouble. They get so anxious to try the fruits of their labor they drink their wine too soon. Wine, like cheese, needs to age a little to develop its best flavor. It's okay to taste the wine before it has completely cleared, and racking is the perfect opportunity, but don't expect it to taste like a finished wine. Judge it too soon and you haven't given it, or yourself, a fair test.

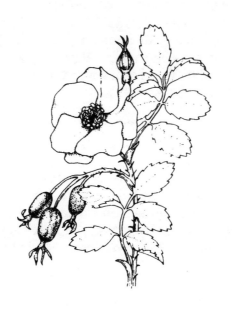

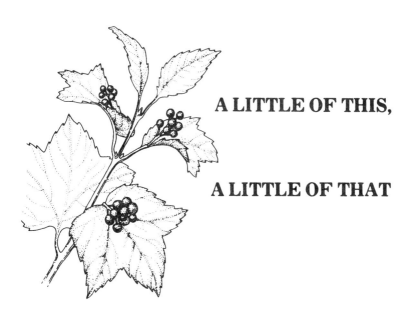

A LITTLE OF THIS,

A LITTLE OF THAT

There's no getting around it. If you are going to be serious about wine making, you are going to need a fair amount of equipment. Fortunately, most of it is relatively inexpensive and easily obtained.

To begin with, you will need plastic pails, jars, or bags for gathering plant material and for holding it during the juice extracting process. Gallon pickle or mayonnaise jars are perfect holding jars. A kitchen scale is also a useful item at this point, since some recipes are given by weight rather than volume. A bottle brush is helpful for cleaning bottles and jars.

Some fruit needs to be cooked to extract its juice. This should be done in an enamel or stainless steel pan. Here is a world of warning: **never** use any other type of metal pan, and **never** allow any metal at all to touch the wine once the yeast has been added. If it happens, the wine is contaminated and must be thrown out.

At this stage, you will also need a wooden spoon for stirring; a plastic colander or sieve and cleen cheesecloth or jelly bag for straining the juice; a wide-mouthed plastic funnel for directing the liquid into the fermentation bottle; a glass fermentation bottle; and an air, or fermentation, lock. Used gallon or four-liter wine bottles make perfect fermentation bottles. For large batches large water cooler bottles are excellent.

After fermentation has stopped and you are ready to transfer the wine for storage, you will need a plastic siphon hose — so you don't stir up the sediment in the bottom of the bottle — a glass storage bottle with a screw-on lid, and sterile cotton balls. Here again, used wine bottles are perfect. The siphon hose should be food-grade plastic, with an inner diameter of ¼-inch to ⅜-inch.

A luxury at this point, but nice if you plan to continue in your avocation of amateur but expert wine maker, is a hydrometer. Hydrometers tell you how much sugar is in the must (the juice, sugar and yeast mixture), what stage fermentation is at when you check it, and the alcohol content of the finished wine.

When the wine is clear and ready for final bottling, you will need your siphon hose, clean and sterilized wine bottles, new wine corks, some heavy paper, and string.

Most of the items needed by the home wine maker, especially at the beginning, are either on hand or readily available at any market or hardware store. More specialized equipment — such as air locks, corks, and yeast — can be found in various specialty stores, from health food shops to garden shops, or can be purchased by catalog.

An equipment check list and a partial list of suppliers can be found at the back of this book.

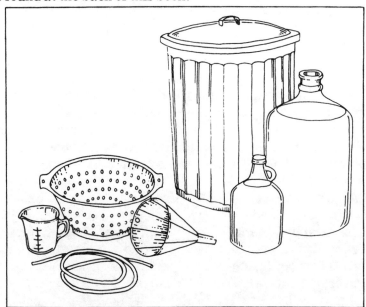

THE WORDS OF WINE

Like any other art, wine making has a language all its own. For the most part, the words are simple and easy to learn, but they can make you sound like a real professional when talking about your hobby.

Air, or fermentation, locks are devices that let carbon dioxide out of the fermentation vessel and keep oxygen and bacteria from getting in. Without an air lock or similar device, pressure from unreleased carbon dioxide could cause the fermentation jar to explode. There are several types of air locks, but they all have two crucial features in common. First, they are attached to a cork that is inserted into the mouth of the fermentation bottle. Second, they all have a place to hold water or sterilizing solution. Bubbles of carbon dioxide can pass through the water, but oxygen and bacteria can't. When the air lock is working, those with moving parts go into action and those without burp. (See figure 1)

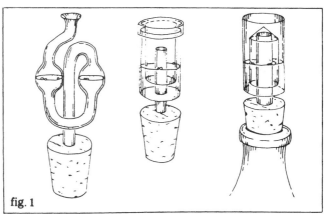

fig. 1

Blending is the process of combining two or more wines to produce finished wines of varying flavors and sweetness. By combining a sweet wine with one that's a little tart, you get one of medium sweetness. You can control the taste and the sweetness by the ratio of one wine to the other. Some wines are a natural blend, such as strawberry and rhubarb, but don't be afraid to experiment. And don't be ashamed to resort to blending. Commercial wine makers do it all the time so they can continue to market a uniform product.

Campden tablets are a form of sulphur dioxide, used to prevent bacteria and oxygen from spoiling your wine with funny flavors, and to preserve color. The usual ratio is one to two tablets per gallon of wine to start. Some people add another tablet at each racking and before bottling. Larger doses — one tablet to each four ounces of water — can be used as a disinfectant for equipment.

Carbon dioxide is produced as a waste product when the yeast converts the sugar to alcohol. Through use of an air lock it is released into the atmosphere, just as it is when you exhale.

Citric acid or citrus fruit juice is used to provide the acid necessary for fermentation in flower wines or wines made from low acid fruits. It also helps the yeast work, stabilizes the wine, and keeps it from developing strange flavors.

Clarifying is another word for letting the wine clear. It takes place during the storage period between fermentation and final bottling of the wine. It may take several months to a year to complete, and may require a second, or even a third, racking.

Cork floggers are specialized tools for seating the cork during the final bottling. There are other ways to make sure the cork is properly seated, but cork floggers are the easiest.

Dextrose is a fine sugar, also called corn sugar, available in specialty shops.

Fermentation is the process in which yeast converts sugar into alcohol. The ideal temperature for fermenting wine is 60°-70° F — much higher and the yeast works itself to death, much lower and it goes to sleep. When fermentation is going on, bubbles can be seen around the top of the must, yeast particles can often be seen rising and falling, and action of the air lock continues.

Fining is a method used to clear up a hazy wine. It calls for sprinkling clean, baked, crushed egg shells over the wine, letting it sit for a day or two, then straining and filtering it.

Flowers of wine is an attractive phrase for an ugly malady. It is an airborne organism that covers the wine with dandruff-like particles. It can be cured by adding Campden tablets if it is caught early, but if a lot of the wine's surface is covered, the whole batch must be thrown out.

Grape tannin is a form of tannic acid found in grape skins. It is used to add body to the wine and enhance its flavor. The usual ratio is one-half teaspoon per gallon. Strong, cold, black tea can be used in its place, but may affect both the color and flavor of the wine.

Hydrometers are specialized tools for measuring the alcohol or sugar content of wine. Once you know that, you can decide what to do to bring the wine more into line with what you want in a finished product.

Lees is the yeast residue at the bottom of the fermenting jar. When transferring the wine from the fermentation vessel to the storage bottle, care must be tken not to disturb the lees so the clarifying wine starts as free from sediment as possible.

Must is the simple word for the juice, sugar and yeast mixture. Sometimes it is also used to refer to the pulp.

Pectin enzyme is added to the must to break down the pectin in fruits. Pectin clouds wine and prevents it from clearing. Pectin enzyme — also called pectolase, pectozyme, and pectinol — should be added when the must is cool as heat kills it. It comes in various forms, with directions for use on the container. Anywhere from a tablet to a tablespoon per gallon is usually sufficient to break down most pectin. A good rule of thumb is to use the smallest amount possible to do the job.

Racking is the official word for siphoning the wine from one jar or bottle to another. Sometimes it is done two or three times to make sure the finished wine is clear.

Sodium, or potassium, metabisulfite is a sterilizer. Mixed in a ratio of ¾ ounce or 336 grains to a gallon of water, the solution is poured into bottles to be used and let stand, covered, for 24 hours. It is not the liquid, generally speaking, but the fumes that do the work, so only a small amount of solution need be used in each bottle. Other equipment may be sterilized by putting it in a covered container with a little bit of the solution. All equipment used in wine making should be sterilized to prevent contamination of the wine by microorganisms. An alternate method of sterilizing bottles is to bake them in an oven at 350° F for one hour. Equipment may be boiled for 10 minutes.

Syrup, a mixture of water and sugar, is sometimes added to the wine while it is still fermenting, to increase its alcohol content or sweetness. The ratio of sugar to water depends on the recipe.

Sweet and dry are the terms used to describe wines. Sweet wines are those that have a relatively high sugar content and taste sweet, although they have a normal alcohol content. Dry wines are those with a low sugar content and no sweet taste. Other terms used to describe wines are **light** and **full-bodied**. Light wines are usually clear and refreshing. They are at their best served chilled. White wines and roses are said to be light, and may be either sweet or dry, or somewhere in between. Full-bodied wines are the red ones, such as Burgundy. They are more robust in flavor and are best served at room temperature. Most red dinner wines are dry; after dinner wines, such as port, are generally sweet.

Topping up is what you do when you add enough boiled water or syrup to the must to fill your container. There is an optimum level for liquid in your fermentation bottle. Too little and the increased amount of air in the bottle increases the possibility of contamination by microorganisms; too much and the froth caused by initial yeast activity may overflow your container. When topping up, always be sure to leave enough head room at the top of the fermentation bottle to contain the foam the exuberant yeast may produce. Fill your jar no higher than its shoulders. (See figure 2) .

fig. 2

Venting is necesary to let carbon dioxide escape from fermenting and storage bottles. Air locks are used to allow venting in the fermentation jar. Sterile cotton balls work well in storage bottles.

Yeast is a living organism that converts sugar and oxygen into alcohol and carbon dioxide. In making wines, only wine yeast should be used. All-purpose wine yeast works well for many wines, but there are other yeasts that can be used to produce specific types of wine. Some of these include: hock or chablis, for dry, light wines, such as those made from flowers; sauterne or tokay, for sweet, light wines; Malaga, Madeira, or sherry, for tawny, sweet wines, such as strawberry; pommard, Burgundy, Bordeaux, or claret, for dry red wines; port, for heavy, sweet red wine; and champagne, for sparkling wines.

Yeast energizer helps the yeast to work. It adds vitamins that may be lacking in the must, particularly when flowers or fruits that are low in vitamin content or have been boiled, dried, or diluted are used. Use about a teaspoon per gallon.

Yeast nutrient contains ammonium salts, which help to break down the albumin, or protein, in the pulp so the yeast can do its job. About half a teaspoon per gallon is sufficient. Yeast nutrient is important in most recipes, but sometimes is replaced by yeast energizer.

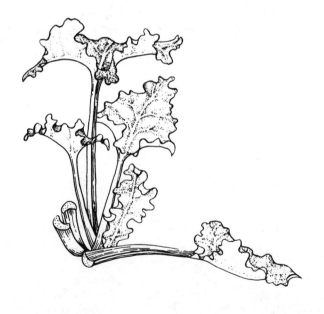

ONE STEP AT A TIME

Once you have made up your mind that you are going to try your hand at wine making and have amassed the supplies you will need to begin, you can start thinking about what you want to use as a base. Wine can be made from almost anything, and in Alaska plant material can be gathered anytime from early spring to late fall.

The gathering expedition can be the most enjoyable part of wine making, for it should be done on a sunny day, and is a great excuse to put your other chores aside and get out of the house.

All material you gather — whether it be flowers, fruit, vegetables, or herbs — should be taken when the plant is young or at its prime. When it looks good is usually the best time to gather it.

Blossoms should be picked when they are in full flower and dry. Only the flower head should be gathered; the green part should be discarded, as it gives the wine a bitter taste. If you are picking flower heads along a state or utility right of way, it's a good idea to find out from the State Department of Transportation or Department of Environmental Conservation whether the area has been sprayed with insecticide or weed killer. If it has, better not pick there. It would not only make your wine taste terrible, it could be dangerous for your health. Plastic gallon jars or plastic food bags make good gathering vessels for flowers.

Fruits or berries should be ripe when they are gathered, but not over ripe. If they're not good to eat, they're not good to drink either. Pint plastic containers are ideal gathering vessels because they can be closed and carried easily in a pack. Also, they are small enough so the fruit isn't crushed by its own weight before you are ready to deal with the juice — a particular hazard with soft berries such as raspberries, salmonberries, or cloudberries.

How much you will need to gather depends both on the type of material you are using and how much wine you want to make. Strong flowers and fruits, such as elderflowers or blueberries, may take as little as a pint for a gallon of wine. Others take as much as a gallon. There is a little leeway here, but if you use too much strong-scented or -flavored material, you'll get a very strong-flavored wine. You can control the flavor of the wine, somewhat, by varying the ratio of flowers or fruit to water and sugar or, after the wine is made, by blending one wine with another. At the beginning, though, it's best to follow the recipe as closely as possible.

Once you have gathered your plant material, hulled it if necessary, and washed it, you start the actual winemaking process. This is the point where you add sugar and/or water to the flower heads or fruit and let the mixture sit — anywhere from a day to a week — stirring it at regular intervals. This produces the juice that is the foundation of your wine. You will need a clean, sterilized container to hold the pulp, a lid or plastic bag to keep air from getting into the mixture, and a wooden spoon for stirring.

The next step is straining the juice from the pulp and putting it into the fermentation jar. For this you will need a sterilized glass or plastic funnel, cheesecloth or jelly bag, glass or plastic dipper, plastic colander, and fermentation bottle. This can be a kind of slow and messy process, but it is important to take as much care with it as possible to avoid getting too much solid material in the fermentation bottle to begin with.

Actually, the process is easy. If you are working with gallons, put your fermenting bottle in the kitchen sink, so that any spillage can be easily cleaned. If you're working with five-gallon jars, put them on the floor atop several layers of paper.

Place your sterilized plastic funnel in the mouth of the fermentation bottle. Over that goes your cheesecloth-lined plastic colander or seive, or your jelly bag. Using your plastic dipper, scoop up as much juice as you can and pour it through the cloth, letting the juice drip through the funnel into the bottle. (See figure 3)

You will have to rinse your cloth or jelly bag in sterilized water fairly often, particularly when you get down toward the end of the pulp, to keep it clear of plant material and allow the juice to flow. Either discard the pulp or — in the case of some strawberry and rhubarb wine recipes — put it aside for freezing or processing for further use.

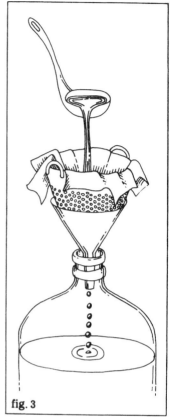

fig. 3

At this point, generally, you add all the other ingredients called for in the recipe. If you need to add more sugar, you may need to do it in the form of a syrup, the ratio of water to sugar depending on the recipe you are using. Yeast can be added right to the must in the bottle, but it is usually a good idea to pour a little must into a plastic or glass dish and sprinkle the yeast onto that. This gives the yeast a good start and gives you an idea of whether it is viable (live) or not. When the yeast froths up it is activated and ready for use. The must should be neither cold nor hot — around 90° F is about right. Too cool, and the yeast will be slow to start too hot, and you kill it. Once the yeast has dissolved, or become foamy, pour it onto the juice in the fermenting bottle.

If your liquid is not quite up to the shoulder of the bottle, top up with a little cool, boiled water, or syrup if you have some left over.

Place a little water or sterilizing solution into the air lock and insert the lock into the mouth of the fermentation bottle.

Label the bottle as to type of wine and date you put it to ferment. Set the bottle in an out-of-the-way spot with a fairly constant temperature of between 60° and 70° F. It is a good idea to set it on several layers of paper in case it overflows. Then sit back and watch it work.

Stage two of the wine making process begins when fermentation has ceased; when no more bubbles are forming and the air lock has stopped working. The wine also looks relatively clear at this point, except for the large amount of sediment, the lees, in the bottom of the bottle. Timing is not critical, but if you leave the wine on the sediment too long after fermentation has stopped, it may develop musty or sharp additions to the flavor.

Now you must transfer the wine from the fermentation bottle to the storage bottle, and this is the tricky part. Being careful not to disturb the lees, set the fermentation bottle on the kitchen counter, table, or other raised platform. You want it to be higher than the bottle or bottles you are going to fill. Remove the air lock and carefully insert the sterilized siphon hose into the wine, keeping it well away from the lees. With the balance of the hose, make a long loop, with the free end being held higher than the fermentation bottle. (See figure 4)

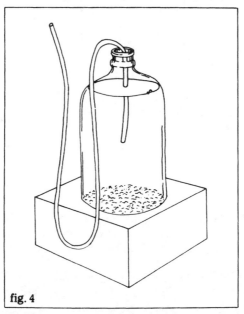

fig. 4

Fold a clean hand around the exposed end of the hose and suck hard, as if you were working on a really thick milkshake. Be sure the hose does not touch your mouth, as this will contaminate the hose and the wine. Stop sucking as soon as the loop in the hose is full.

The first liquid through the hose should be discarded, as it may carry a residue of your sterlizing solution. The rest goes into the storage bottles. You may want to put a little in a glass for tasting, too, as this is the perfect opportunity to see what kind of wine you are going to get.

How fast the liquid runs from one container to the next during the racking depends on the diameter of your hose and how high or low one end of the hose is in relation to the other. As the end in the storage jar is raised, the flow slows down; if it is raised too far, flow may stop altogether and you may have to start the siphoning process all over again.

Transferring the wine is a good job for two people, although it can be done by one. You have to keep an eye on both bottles and control both ends of the hose at the same time, to make sure you don't disturb the lees and don't spill your wine.

Once the fluid level passes the shoulders of your storage jar, you need to slow the rate of flow quickly so you don't have an overflow. (See figure 5) You need to leave a little space at the

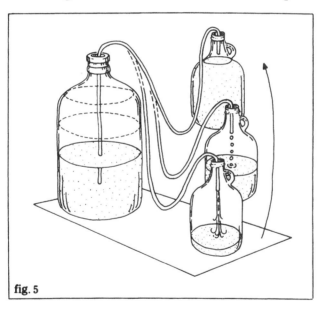

fig. 5

top of the storage jar, but not as much as you needed for fermentation. As long as the neck of the bottle is clear, you are okay. However, if you have too much space, you take the chance of bacterial contamination from the increased amount of air in the container. If you have too much space, top up with cool, boiled water.

As the fluid level in the fermentation bottle decreases, your hose gets closer and closer to the lees. When you can see the sediment is beginning to get stirred up, stop siphoning.

Place a sterile cotton ball in the mouth of the storage bottle, put the lid on and screw it shut, then unscrew it slightly so that it is not tightly sealed. This is necessary so that venting can continue, and is a good safeguard against explosion should fermentation start up again, as it sometimes does after racking.

Label your bottle as to type of wine and the date of first racking. Put it in a cool, darkened area, such as a root cellar, and let it sit for a couple of months to a year, until it is clear. Storage temperature for wines should be a steady 40°-60° F, although 50°-55° F is best. The key word is steady. A place that is cool in winter but heats up in the summer, or that is cool at night but warm in the daytime, is not good for wine storage.

After about three months, check your wine, and if it has thrown another sediment rack it again. Repeat this process until the wine is absolutely clear. You won't have terrible wine if you don't rack it more than once, but it probably will be clearer and better tasting if you do. Of course, each racking gives you another opportunity to taste test your wine and see how it is improving.

Once the wine is clear, the third stage of wine making begins. This is when you transfer it from the storage container into the bottle or bottles you will use for long-term storage. The process is basically the same as for the second stage, the racking. The wine is carefully siphoned into sterilized bottles. You can do this on an as-needed basis, or you can go the whole route and bottle your wine like the professionals. This is the best way to go about it if you intend to keep the wine for long periods of time or give it as gifts, and avoids the necessity of having to reach for the siphon hose every time you want a bottle of wine.

This final stage of wine making is when blending should be done. If you haven't already tasted your wine — although you would be an unusual wine maker if you haven't — now is the time to do so.

In blending wines, you may have to experiment a little with the ratio of one wine to another to get the flavor and taste you want. This depends on how sweet or dry your wines are to start, and how sweet or dry you want the finished wine to be. Make fairly precise measurements when experimenting and keep track of the one which works best with the wines you are blending. Duplicate that ratio when you put the wine into the bottles.

When you have filled a bottle midway up its neck, put it

aside for corking. Continue filling bottles until you have used all your wine. It is as important at this stage as at any of the others not to let too much air space remain between the wine and the mouth of the bottle. But, unlike the other stages, you won't be topping up with water now. If you don't have enough wine to fill a bottle fully, choose a smaller bottle, or decant it for drinking soon. Don't try to store wine for long periods in anything but full bottles.

After the bottles are full, you must cork them. Corking requires three things: clean, sterilized, new or used but intact corks; about eight inches of very thin stainless steel wire affixed to a length of dowling; and some way to seat the cork straight and securely. If you are really going to get into wine making, a cork flogger is ideal. It looks a little like a bottle capper and uses leverage to force the cork into the bottle.

The purpose of the wire is to let air out as you seat the cork. As the cork goes in, it compresses the air inside and a lot of pressure builds up. At worst, the pressure can break the bottle, wasting all your effort to that point. At best, it can force the cork back out, and you'll have to cork the bottle all over again.

fig. 6

Insert the sterilized wire into the mouth of the bottle along one side. Place the cork in the bottle and — if you don't use a flogger — either push it against the wall, using your body as a base for the bottle, or put a flat surface on top of the cork and force it down, making sure the bottle is held securely so it doesn't tip. (See figure 6)

Once the cork is seated slightly below the mouth of the bottle (no more than ⅛-inch), gradually pull the wire out. An extra step at this point, which isn't necessary but is a nice finishing touch, is to seal the cork with a little melted paraffin.

Next, cut a three-inch square of heavy paper, such as butcher paper or freeze wrap. Fold it down over the top of the bot-

29

tle and tie it closed with stiff twine or wire. This protects the seal and keeps it free from dust and mold, something you and your friends will appreciate when it comes time to pour the wine.

Label each bottle as to type of wine and date of bottling and put in a cool, dark place for storage. Temperature conditions for final storage are the same as for interim storage: 40°-60° F, with 50°-55° F being optimum.

Corked bottles should be stored on their sides to keep the corks moist. This avoids shrinking and possible contamination by airborne bacteria.

At this point, all your work is finished. All you have to do is enjoy the wine and your friends' reactions to it. That little old wine maker of legend is you.

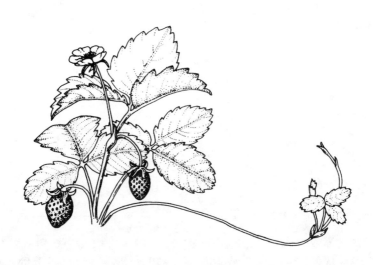

WHAT CAN GO WRONG

Home wine making is an art, not a science. Conditions vary, and mistakes occur. But armed with a little knowledge of what can go wrong and what can be done about it, you can still produce high quality wine almost every time.

Prevention, of course, is always preferable to a curative. So, to begin with, make sure that everything that comes in contact with your wine, from start to finish, is clean and sterilized. Contamination is probably the main source of problems for home wine makers. So, be clean, and be careful.

Of course, problems may crop up for other reasons.

Sometimes fermentation stops before it has done its job of converting sugar to alcohol. The first thing to do when fermentation "sticks" is nothing. Many times patience alone can cure the problem, and fermentation will begin again on its own after a month or two. If it does not, all is not lost, for there are several other remedies to try.

Adding too much sugar to the must at the beginning sometimes overwhelms the yeast. If you think that is what might have happened, dilute the must by adding a pint or two of cool, boiled water.

Other possibilities to keep in mind are lack of adequate nutrient — in which case you add a little yeast energizer — or poor temperature control. Remember that temperature regulates what the yeast does. If your fermentation jar is set in too cool a location, fermentation may stop. On the other hand, too high a temperature kills the yeast. If you think you've killed your yeast, make a fresh yeast starter and add it to the must.

Once in awhile, a fermenting wine develops a haze. This can be due to too much pectin, too much starch, or to metal contamination. If you think the latter may be the cause, a slight haze can be cleared by adding a small amount of citric acid. But if the haze is pronounced, there's no remedy but to throw the wine away.

To clear a pectin haze, of course, add a teaspoon of pectozyme to the must and let it stand in a warm place for several days. Then, bake cleaned, empty egg shells until they're brittle, crush them, and scatter the particles on the wine surface. This process is called fining. After a day or two, strain and filter the wine. Fining can also clear up a starch-produced haze.

If your finished wine looks thick and oily and pours slowly, it is said to be ropy. Sometimes ropiness can be cured by simply racking the wine into a clean and sterilized bottle. If this approach doesn't work, add two crushed Campden tablets to the wine, stir it vigorously, then filter the wine into a clean, sterilized bottle.

Other problems with finished wine may be flatness, over-sweetness, or mustiness. If your wine tastes flat, add a little grape tannin and let the wine sit for awhile. If it is too sweet, add a small amount of citric acid or lemon juice and aerate the wine by pouring it quickly back and forth between clean, sterilized containers. Or, you can blend it with a wine that is a little too dry.

Mustiness, caused by allowing the wine to stand too long on the lees before racking it, is incurable. You can blend a musty wine with a better tasting one, but the resulting blend will still retain a musty flavor.

Perhaps the nastiest problem that can beset your wine is one that has the loveliest name: flowers of wine. This is a yeast-like organism that floats on top of the wine like flakes of dandruff and converts it to carbon dioxide and water, with acetic acid as a by-product. It is an airborne disease, made possible by leaving too much space in your storage bottle. If you catch the problem early and contamination is slight, it may be cured by adding two Campden tablets to the wine and then filtering it carefully into a fresh, clean, sterilized bottle. However, if the "flowers" cover the wine surface, the disease has gone too far and the wine is beyond rescue. Throw it out.

In wine making, if you are methodical, scrupulously clean, and follow directions, you should have few problems to contend with later on. Take time at the beginning and every step along the way, and you'll save time in the long run.

FROM START

TO FINISH

All anyone needs in order to become a successful wine maker is a source of plant material, a few supplies, a little dedication, a lot of patience, and some good recipes. The recipes in this book have all been tried and tested, either by me or by some other home wine maker. Recipes from my kitchen are marked with an asterisk (*).

To help you find the recipe you want without having to thumb through an index, I have entered the recipes alphabetically. Unless otherwise specified, all recipes are intended to make one gallon of wine. To increase that amount, simply multiply your ingredients, except the yeast, by the number of gallons you desire.

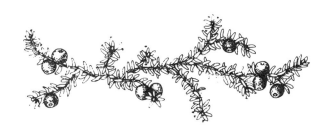

Blueberry (Bilberry) Wine*

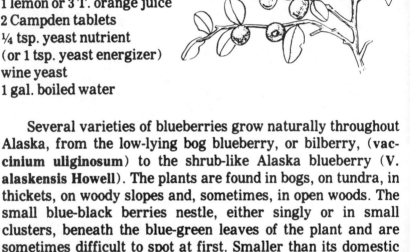

1½ lb. blueberries
2 lb. sugar
1 lemon or 3 T. orange juice
2 Campden tablets
¼ tsp. yeast nutrient
(or 1 tsp. yeast energizer)
wine yeast
1 gal. boiled water

Several varieties of blueberries grow naturally throughout Alaska, from the low-lying bog blueberry, or bilberry, (vaccinium uliginosum) to the shrub-like Alaska blueberry (V. alaskensis Howell). The plants are found in bogs, on tundra, in thickets, on woody slopes and, sometimes, in open woods. The small blue-black berries nestle, either singly or in small clusters, beneath the blue-green leaves of the plant and are sometimes difficult to spot at first. Smaller than its domestic cousin, our dusky Alaskan berry, nontheless, surpasses it in flavor. In fact, the berry is so strong it is easy to use too much in making wine. Very little is needed to give color, flavor and body; more than a little can be overpowering. Blueberries make a heavy red wine.

Pick your blueberries on a sunny day. If you don't have time to start your wine yet, that's okay because blueberries store and freeze well.

Wash and weigh 1½ pounds of blueberries. Pour over them four pints of boiling water and crush. Add two pounds of sugar, stirring until it is dissolved. Cool the mixture until it is about body temperature. Place a little of the mixture in a small bowl, sprinkle the wine yeast over it, and let sit until frothy. To the rest of the mixture, add ¼ tsp. yeast nutrient (or 1 tsp. yeast energizer), two crumbled Campden tablets, the juice of one lemon, or three tablespoons of orange juice, and the activated yeast.

Pour the mixture into a clean, sterilized jar, cover it with plastic, and put a lid on it but do not seal it. Ferment the wine on the pulp for one week, stirring one or two times a day with a wooden spoon. Strain the mixture and transfer the liquid to your fermenting jar. Top up with cool, boiled water and close the container with an air lock. Set in a warm place until fermentation is completed. Rack your wine and set it in a cool, dark place for storage until it clears, racking again as needed. Siphon into sterilized bottles, cork, and store in a cool, dark place.

Cloudberry Wine

I have never been able to gather enough cloudberries to make even a gallon of wine, but the succulent, apricot-colored berry is said to grow profusely in many parts of the state and is found in boggy areas and tundra . Related to the rose, the cloudberry (**Rubus chamaemorus**) has a flavor reminiscent of baked apples and is very high in vitamin C. If you are fortunate enough to find an abundance of these lovely berries and feel like experimenting, try the recipe for rosehip wine or strawberry wine.

Clover Wine*
(Makes Five Gallons)

14 quarts flowerheads
20 T. lemon juice
20 T. orange juice
4 tsp. lemon rind
4 tsp. orange rind
10 lb. sugar
wine yeast
water

Clover is not native to Alaska, but it grows well here and is often used as a ground cover, particularly along road cuts or rights of way. Clover makes a light, clear wine with a very subtle aroma. Many home wine makers say the best clover for wine is pink clover, which bears large, heavily scented, deep pink blossoms. But the most common clover in Alaska bears small, light pink or white blossoms that are less heavily scented than the larger variety. They, too make good wine.

Gather your clover on a dry, preferably sunny, day. Pick only the flower heads, making sure no part of the stem is attached. Do not wait longer than a day or two to start your wine, as the flowers wilt fairly quickly.

Measure the flower heads loosely and place in a container big enough to hold several gallons. Dissolve the sugar in three gallons of water and bring to a boil; cool. Pour fruit juices and rind over flowers. Pour cooled syrup over all. Add cool, boiled water to bring the volume to four or five gallons. Add wine yeast, previously mixed with a little of the lukewarm syrup. Stir, cover, and set to ferment on flower heads for seven days, stirring daily. Strain liquid into fermentation bottle and add enough boiled, cool water to bring the volume to five gallons. Insert air lock and let ferment to a finish. Rack and store in a cool, dark place until clear. Rack, bottle, cork, and store in a cool, dark place.

Clover Wine No. 2*

¾ - 1 gal. flower heads, loosely measured
2-3 lb. sugar
juice from 2 lemons and two oranges
(or 3 tsp. citric acid)
1 Campden tablet
½ tsp. grape tannin
½ lb. raisins, chopped
½ tsp. yeast energizer
wine yeast
1 gal. boiled water

Rinse blossoms and place in a large bowl. Add water, raisins, sugar, Campden tablet, citrus juice (or citric acid) and rind. Cool to lukewarm. Activate yeast in a little warm water and add to mixture; add yeast energizer. Pour into a clean, sterilized container and cover loosely. Ferment on pulp for three days, stirring daily. Strain liquid into fermentation bottle, top up with cool, boiled water, and close with an air lock. Place in a warm spot and ferment to a finish. Rack and store in a cool, dark place until clear. Rack into sterilized bottles, cork, and store in a cool, dark place until used.

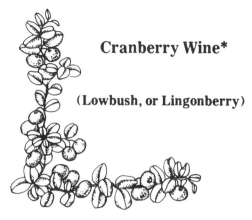

Cranberry Wine*

(Lowbush, or Lingonberry)

3-4 lb. cranberries
2½-3 lb. sugar
½ lb. raisins, chopped
1 Campden tablet
½ tsp. yeast nutrient
pectin enzyme
wine yeast
water

Of the two varieties of true cranberries that grow in Alaska, the lowbush, or lingonberry, (**Vaccinium vitis idaea**) is the most prolific. It is found throughout most of the state, in rocky or peaty, acidic soil. It likes dry spruce forests or overburned areas especially. As its name implies, the plant grows low to the ground. The tiny leaves are leathery and shiny green. The berry, bright to deep red in color, grows singly or in small clusters, and the contrast of red against green makes it easily seen. Much smaller than its domestic cousin, the lowbush cranberry far surpasses it in flavor. It makes a light, clear, red wine.

Gather the berries in the fall, preferably after the first frost. Cranberries store and freeze well, and can be kept for months, if necessary, until you are able to make your wine.

Wash and weigh the berries. Pour enough boiling water over the fruit to cover it. Mash the berries and add raisins. Add the sugar, stirring to dissolve. Cool to slightly more than lukewarm. Use a small amount of the liquid to activate the yeast and set aside until frothy. Add the yeast nutrient and pectin enzyme to the rest of the juice. Add the activated yeast and enough cool, boiled water to make up to one gallon of liquid. Place in a loosely covered container and ferment on the pulp for a week, stirring daily. Strain the liquid into a fermentation bottle, top up with cool, boiled water if necessary, insert air lock, and set to ferment in a warm place. Rack, store in a cool, dark place until clear, then rack again and bottle.

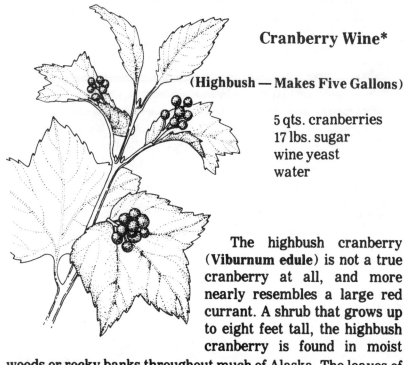

Cranberry Wine*

(Highbush — Makes Five Gallons)

5 qts. cranberries
17 lbs. sugar
wine yeast
water

The highbush cranberry (**Viburnum edule**) is not a true cranberry at all, and more nearly resembles a large red currant. A shrub that grows up to eight feet tall, the highbush cranberry is found in moist woods or rocky banks throughout much of Alaska. The leaves of this plant are broad and crinkly, with rounded lobes, and look sort of like a soft-edged maple leaf. The berries grow in clusters of round, red drupelets and are translucent when ripe, in late fall. The berry has a musty, almost rancid, odor and is highly acid, but makes a very dry, clear, light red wine.

Wash berries to remove leaf and stem particles. Bring three quarts of water to a boil and pour over cranberries. Let cool to body temperature and mash with a wooden spoon. Let set in a covered container for four days, stirring daily. Strain onto 10 lb. of sugar, add enough boiled water to bring the liquid content to four gallons, and stir well. Place a small amount of the liquid in a small bowl, sprinkle the yeast on top of it, and as soon as it becomes frothy, return it to the rest of the mixture. Cover and let ferment for 24 hours. Pour into fermentation bottle, insert air lock, and set in warm place to ferment. When fermentation has slowed down, make a syrup of 7 lb. of sugar and one gallon water. Add to fermenting liquid, replace air lock, and ferment to a finish. Rack and store in a cool, dark place until clear. Rack again, bottle, and store.

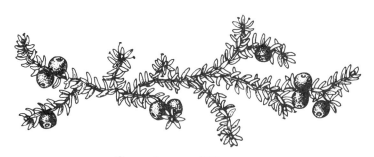

Crowberry Wine

5 lb. crowberries	wine yeast
¼ c. lemon juice	1 gal. water

Crowberries (**Empetrum nigrum**), also called blackberries or curlewberries, are a small, low-lying plant found in wet or boggy areas throughout the state. The leaves are needle-like, resembling juniper needles. The berry, which is shiny and dark blue to black in color, grows either singly or in clusters along the small branches. They are best picked in the fall.

Place berries in a crock. Boil the water and pour over the berries. Crush well. Cover the crock with a clean cloth and let it stand five days, stirring twice daily. Strain liquid, discarding the pulp. Add lemon juice and sugar. Sprinkle yeast over the surface and stir well. Cover the crock and let stand for three days. Siphon liquid into a fermentation bottle, insert an air lock, and let ferment to a finish. Rack and store in a cool, dark place until cleared. Rack again and bottle.

Currant Wine

The best Alaska currant to use for wine is the American red currant (**Ribes triste Pallas.**). It is said to grow abundantly in cool woods and swampy areas throughout the state, although I have never been lucky enough to gather more than a handful. A shrub with stems up to five feet high, the currant has broad, toothed and lobed leaves. The fruit, grown on old stalks in one- to two-inch long clusters, is bright red and transluscent when ripe. If you find enough of this astringent fruit and want to experiment, try the recipe for highbush cranberry wine.

Dandelion Wine*

1 gal. dandelion petals	2 lb. sugar
juice and rind of 1 orange and 1 lemon	wine yeast
(or equivalents)	water

Native to Alaska or not, the dandelion (**Taraxacum officinale**) is found everywhere. A hardy plant, it is one of the first to bloom in the spring and can often be seen rearing its sunny head long after all other vegetation has quit for the winter. The dandelion (from the French **dent de lion**, or lion's tooth, for its toothed leaves) is a truly versatile plant. Its leaves can be used raw in salads or cooked as a spinach-like vegetable, its root can be roasted and ground for use as a coffee substitute, and its flowers make a delectable, light, clear wine.

Gather the blossoms on a bright, sunny day in spring or early summer, when the flower heads are fully open. Be sure to discard any stem or green parts, as these are very bitter.

Place flower heads in a container. Pour over them one gallon of boiling water, and stir. Cover and set aside for two to three days, stirring daily. Strain into a large enamel or stainless steel pan and bring juice to a boil with the fruit rinds. Simmer for 10 minutes and strain onto the sugar and stir. When the must is lukewarm, add the fruit juice and activated yeast. Place in a fermentation bottle, top up with boiled water if necessary, insert air lock, and place in a warm spot to ferment to a finish. Rack and store in a cool place for several months until clear. Rack again and bottle.

Dandelion Wine No. 2*
(Makes Five Gallons)

3 gal. flower heads
15 lbs. sugar
4 Campden tablets, crushed
2 lb. raisins, chopped
15 tsp. citric acid

2½ tsp. yeast energizer
2 tsp. grape tannin
wine yeast
water

Place flower heads in a large container and pour 2½ gallons of boiling water over them. Cover and let sit for two to three days, stirring daily. Prepare a syrup, using 2½ gallons of boiling water and the sugar. Add to flower heads along with the rest of the ingredients, including activated yeast, and ferment on the flower heads for three days. Strain into a fermentation bottle, top up if necessary, insert air lock, and place in a warm spot to ferment to a finish. Rack and store in a cool, dark place until clear. Rack and bottle.

Dandelion Wine No. 3*

2 qts. flower heads
2 lbs. sugar
½ lb. raisins, chopped
juice of 2 lemons and 2 oranges
(or equivalent)

1 Campden tablet
½ tsp. grape tannin
½ tsp. yeast nutrient
wine yeast
water

Place flower heads in a container and cover with a syrup made by dissolving half the sugar in a gallon of boiling water. Stir in the Campden tablet, cover and let sit for 24 hours. Strain half the liquid into an enamel or stainless steel pan and heat. Pour the heated liquid over the remainder of the sugar and stir until dissolved. Cool to body temperature. Add, along with the remainder of the ingredients and activated wine yeast, to the flower liquid. Cover and let sit for five days, stirring twice daily. Strain and transfer liquid to a fermentation bottle. Top up with cool, boiled water, insert air lock, and ferment to a finish in a warm place. Rack and store in a cool, dark place until clear. Rack again and bottle.

Elderberry Wine

2 gal. elderberries
1 gal. water
4 lb. brown sugar
1 oz. whole cloves
2 oz. ginger pieces
yeast

The red-berried elder (**Sambucus racemosa**) is a medium to tall shrub found throughout most of Southeastern, Southcentral, and Southwestern Alaska. The flowers grow in large, pyramidal clusters at the end of branches. By early fall the flowers have given way to clusters of bright red berries, much prized by migrating birds.

There is some disagreement over whether the berry is edible. Some digestive upsets have been reported, and some authorities consider the berries poisonous. Anyone with a sensitive stomach or history of allergies probably should avoid this berry.

The flowers have quite a strong scent and make a good foundation for wine. Elderflower wine is light and clear with a spicy, woody bouquet.

Pick elderberries on a sunny day. Wash and measure. Pour one gallon of water over the berries and let stand for 40 hours. Bring mixture to a slow boil for one hour. Strain and add sugar, cloves, and ginger. Boil slowly for about 15 minutes. Cool to body temperature, activate yeast and add. Transfer must to fermentation bottle, top up with cool, boiled water if necessary, insert air lock, and ferment to a finish. Rack and store in a cool, dark place until clear. Rack again and bottle.

Elderberry Wine No. 2

1 gal. elderberries

6-12 c. sugar

wine yeast

water

Wash berries and place in an enamel pan with about a quart of water; bring to a boil and cook until berries burst. Mash them and pour pulp into a cloth sack. Drip out the juice by letting hang overnight. Do not squeeze sack. Pour juice into fermenting jar and add sugar to taste. Top up with cool, boiled water. Set the whole jar in a deep pan of warm water and bring the temperature of the must up to lukewarm. Sprinkle one-fifth of the yeast package into the juice. Remove the jar from the water, insert air lock, and set in a warm place to ferment. Rack and store in a cool, dark place until clear. Repeat racking as needed to free wine from the yellow scum that may form. Rack one last time and bottle.

Elderflower Wine No. 1*

2 pts. flowerets

1 Campden tablet

½ tsp. yeast nutrient

¼ tsp. grape tannin

3 tsp. citric acid

2 lbs. sugar

2 T. lemon juice

wine yeast

water

Pour boiling water on flowerets and stir. Add all ingredients except yeast and energizer. When must is body temperature, add yeast and energizer. Cover and ferment on flowerets for three days. Strain liquid into fermentation bottle, insert air lock, and ferment to a finish in a warm spot. Rack and store in a cool, dark place to clear. Rack again and bottle.

Elderflower Wine No. 2*

1 pt. flowerets

juice and rind of 2 lemons

(or equivalent)

3 lb. sugar

wine yeast

water

Pour ½-⅔ gallon of boiling water over flowerets and thinly peeled lemon rind (or equivalent in powdered rind). Cover and set aside for three days, stirring daily.   Strain onto sugar and bring to a boil. Simmer for 10 minutes. Cool to body heat and place in a fermentation bottle. Add lemon juice, wine yeast, and cool, boiled water to top up. Insert air lock and place in a warm spot to ferment to a finish. Rack and store in a cool, dark place until clear. Rack again and bottle.

Nagoonberry Wine

Nagoonberries (**Rubus arcticus**), also called wine berries, are deep red berries of the blackberry type that, like strawberries, grow close to the ground. Their bright deep-rose pink flowers are evident in late spring and early summer, and the berries are available in late summer or early fall. Nagoonberries have an indescribably delicious taste and should make excellent wine of a clear, light red variety. Unfortunately, the berry is not usually found in great abundance, and since you can expect to use about a gallon of berries to a gallon of water, you may wish to save any you do find for other delights. If you have enough and want to try a wine, use the recipe for strawberry wine.

Nettle Wine
(Makes Four Gallons)

3 gallons nettles
4 gallons water
10 lb. sugar
yeast

Stinging nettles (**Urtica lyallii**) are among the first plants to emerge in the spring. They love moist ground and grow profusely along or near streambeds and springs, and have a particular fondness for

44

roadsides and paths. The plants, which ultimately grow to almost six feet high, should be picked in early spring, when they are no taller than three to six inches. Wear gloves while picking them, since they really can sting.

Place nettles in a crock. Boil four gallons of water and pour over the nettles. Add sugar and stir until it dissolves. Cool to body heat and add yeast. Cover the crock and allow mixture to stand for five days, stirring occasionally. Siphon liquid into fermentation bottle or bottles, top up with cool, boiled water if necessary, insert air lock, and place in a warm spot to ferment to a finish. After about 10 weeks, rack and store in a cool, dark place until clear. After four months, rack again and bottle. Matures in six months.

Raspberry Wine

1½-3 lb. raspberries
2-2½ lb. sugar
2 Campden tablets
pectin enzyme
½ tsp. yeast nutrient
wine yeast
water

Red raspberries (**Rubus idaeus**) grow profusely throughout coastal Alaska and up into the Matanuska Valley, the Alaska Range, and the Yukon River district. Its domestic cousin is also one of Alaska's most successful garden fruits. The wild raspberry grows on canes up to four feet tall and only appears on second-year plants. The berry has a sharper, more defined taste than the garden variety and makes a wonderful clear, red wine.

Cover raspberries with four pints boiling water. Add sugar and two pints of cold water and stir until sugar is dissolved. Add Campden tablets and yeast nutrient and stir. Cool mixture to body heat, add pectin enzyme and activated yeast. Cover and ferment on pulp for one week, stirring daily. Strain into fermentation bottle, top up with boiled water if necessary, insert air lock, and set in a warm place to ferment to a finish. Rack and store in a cool, dark place until clear. Rack again and bottle.

Raspberry Wine No. 2

Enough raspberries to
make ½ gallon juice
3-6 c. sugar

½ gal. water
wine yeast

Pick very ripe berries clean enough so they don't need to be washed. Mash and put them in a cloth sack. Drip out the juice by letting it hang overnight. Do not squeeze the sack. Put the juice into a sterilized fermentation jar and add sugar according to how sweet you want the wine to be. Add cool, boiled water to top up. Set the whole jar in a deep pan of water and bring the temperature of the juice up to lukewarm. Sprinkle one-fifth package of yeast into the juice. Remove the jar from the water, insert air lock, and place in a warm spot to ferment to a finish. After four to eight weeks, when fermenting has stopped, rack and store in a cool, dark place until clear. Rack again and bottle. This wine was a first-place winner at the Alaska State Fair in Ninilchik.

Rhubarb Wine*

3 lb. diced rhubarb
2-3 lb. sugar
1 Campden tablet, crushed

1 tsp. yeast nutrient
wine yeast
1 gal. water

Rhubarb is not a native to Alaska, but it grows very successfully in most northern gardens. Because it keeps growing even as it is cut, it is easy to gather enough of the fruit to make five or even 10 gallons of wine. Only the stalk should be gathered, as the leaves and root of this herb are poisonous.

Wash the rhubarb and cut off all soft or bad spots. Cut

stalks into ½- to 1-inch chunks. Put a layer of rhubarb in a container and cover with a layer of sugar. Continue layering, ending with a sugar layer, until all rhubarb and sugar has been used. Cover and let sit for at least 24 hours, until all the sugar has dissolved. Strain juice into a fermentation bottle. Rinse rhubarb with cool, boiled water and strain again. Add strained liquid to juice in fermenting bottle. (The rhubarb can be frozen for use in cooking later, although recipes should be adjusted to use less sugar than called for.) Add crushed Campden tablet, yeast nutrient, and wine yeast to liquid in fermentation jar. Add cool, boiled water to top up. Insert air lock and set in a warm place to ferment to a finish. Rack and store in a cool, dark place until clear. Rack again, cork, and bottle.

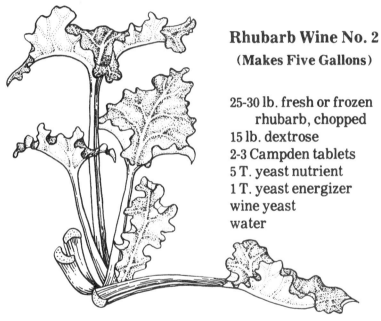

Rhubarb Wine No. 2
(Makes Five Gallons)

25-30 lb. fresh or frozen
    rhubarb, chopped
15 lb. dextrose
2-3 Campden tablets
5 T. yeast nutrient
1 T. yeast energizer
wine yeast
water

Layer rhubarb and dextrose in a large container or in five gallon buckets. Set aside for 24 hours to draw out juice. Drain and set liquid aside. Cover rhubarb with cool, boiled water and let sit for one hour. Drain and add liquid to the juice previously set aside. Fill fermentation jar three-quarters full, adding water if necessary. Add Campden tablets, yeast nutrient, yeast energizer, and yeast. Cover and let fermentation begin, then top up with cool, boiled water or reserved juice. Insert air lock and ferment to a finish. Rack and store in a cool, dark place. Rack three times during storage, then bottle after a year.

Rhubarb Wine No. 3

3 lb. rhubarb
6 c. sugar
wine yeast
3 qts. water, or enough to make
    a gallon of juice

Cut rhubarb into ½-inch pieces. Pour boiling water over fruit and set aside overnight. Pour into a cloth sack and drip out juice by letting it hang overnight. Do not squeeze sack and do not add any more water. Pour liquid into fermentation jar and add sugar and yeast. Insert air lock and set in a warm place to ferment to a finish. Rack and store in a cool, dark place until clear. Rack again and bottle.

Rose Hip Wine

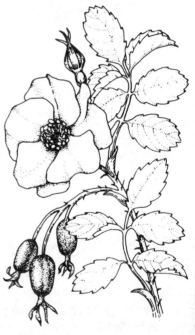

5 lb. rose hips
1 lb. raisins
2 lemons
3½ lb. sugar
1 gal. water
yeast

The prickly rose (**Rosa acicularis Lindl.**) grows everywhere in Alaska. Beautiful to look at, a wild rose is a real treasure house for wine makers. The petals, gathered on sunny summer days, make an exquisitely scented, clear, pale pink wine. The fruit, plucked in the cool crisp of autumn, makes a tawny wine.

The "hip" is the fruit of the plant, the part of the flower that's left on the bush after the petals drop. When ripe, it tastes a little like an apple. It is very high in vitamin C. Rose hips are also high in pectin, and although this recipe does not call for pectin enzyme, it would be a good addition.

Pick rose hips in the fall, when they are red and fairly firm. Wash them and grind them up with raisins and lemons. Put the mixture into a crock or other container and cover with boiling water. Cover and let stand for four days. Strain liquid into a clean container and discard the solids. Add sugar to the liquid and stir until it is dissolved. Sprinkle yeast over the surface of the must, cover the container, and let stand for four days. Siphon into fermentation bottle, top up with cool, boiled water if necessary, insert air lock, and ferment to a finish in a warm place. Rack and place in a cool, dark storage area for three months. Rack again and store for another three months. Repeat once more. Rack and bottle.

Spiced Rose Hip Wine

4 lb. ripe rose hips	3 lb. sugar
1 lemon, thinly sliced	yeast
1½ T. whole cloves	water
3 cinnamon sticks	

Wash rose hips well, crush with a mallet, and put in a crock. Pour one quart boiled water over fruit. Boil 1½ lb. sugar in one quart water for two minutes. Cool 10 minutes, then add lemon and spices. Add syrup to rose hips and mix well. Add yeast and cover crock. Let ferment on pulp one week. Strain liquid into clean container and discard solids. Boil 1½ lb. sugar in three quarts of water for four minutes. Cool 20 minutes and add to rose hip liquor. Cover and let ferment for another week. Strain into fermentation bottle, top up with cool, boiled water if necessary, insert air lock, and let ferment to a finish in a warm place. Rack and store in a cool, dark place until clear. Rack again and bottle.

Rose Petal Wine No. 1*
(Makes Five Gallons)

14 qts. rose petals	5 tsp. powdered lemon peel
15 lb. sugar	wine yeast
20 T. lemon juice	water

Dissolve sugar in about four gallons of water. Add

powdered lemon peel and bring to a boil. Let cool, then pour over petals and juice. Stir well. Add yeast, mixed with a little of the lukewarm liquid. Cover well and let ferment on petals for seven days, stirring daily. Strain off into a fermentation bottle. Top up with cool, boiled water, insert air lock, and set in a warm place to ferment to a finish. Rack and store in a cool, dark place until clear. Rack again and bottle.

Rose Petal Wine No. 2*
(Makes Five Gallons)

10 qts. rose petals
10 lb. sugar
10 Campden tablets
1¼ c. citrus juice
5 tablets yeast nutrient
wine yeast
water

Stir rose petals into 3⅓ gallons boiling water. Cover and let sit for 24 hours. Strain into fermentation bottle. Dissolve sugar in one gallon of water and bring to a boil. Cool. Break nutrient and Campden tablets into citrus juice. Add to rose water in fermentation bottle. Add syrup to mixture. Add yeast and top up with cool, boiled water. Insert air lock and set in a warm place to ferment to a finish. Rack and store in a cool, dark place until clear. Rack again and bottle.

Rose Petal Wine No. 3

1 lb. rose petals
1 gal. water
4 lb. sugar
2 lemons, sliced
yeast

Boil the petals in water, then pour over the sugar and stir. Add the lemons and yeast. Cover and let ferment on the petals for one week, stirring daily. Strain into fermentation bottle, insert air lock, and let ferment to a finish. Rack and store in a cool, dark place until clear. Rack again and bottle.

Rose Petal Wine No. 4

1 qt. rose petals
juice of one lemon
4 c. dextrose
wine yeast

1 gal. water
1 tablet yeast nutrient
1 tsp. yeast energizer
1 Campden tablet

Stir the petals into one gallon of boiling water. Cover and let sit for 24 hours. Strain. Add the lemon juice, yeast nutrient, yeast energizer, dextrose, Campden tablet, and wine yeast. Pour into fermentation jar, insert air lock, and let ferment to a finish. Rack and place in a cool, dark place. Repeat racking twice more. Bottle after one year.

Salmonberry Wine

1½ gal. crushed salmonberries
1 gal. water
4 lb. sugar
yeast

Salmonberries grow on shrubs to six feet in height and are found in Southeastern Alaska and along the Alaskan Gulf coast. Related to the rose, the salmonberry (**Rubus spectabilis**) somewhat resembles a boysenberry, except for its color. When ripe, in late summer or early fall, it is translucent and either yellow or bright red.

Place berries in a crock. Pour water over them and crush. Cover crock and let stand five days. Stir in sugar; cover and let stand for one week more. Strain juice, squeezing pulp as dry as possible. Discard solids. Return juice to a clean container; cover and let stand three days. Siphon must into a fermentation bottle, add yeast, insert air lock, and let ferment to a finish — about three months. Rack and store in a cool, dark place until clear. Rack again and bottle.

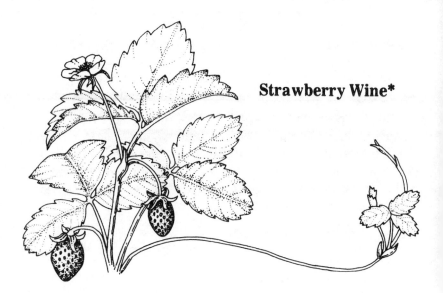

Strawberry Wine*

4 lb. strawberries
2½ lb. sugar
1 Campden tablet, crushed
1 T. citric acid
½ tsp. yeast energizer

½ tsp. grape tannin
1 tsp. pectin enzyme
wine yeast
1 gal. boiled water

Strawberries do grow wild in Alaska, but my experience has been that they are few and far between. Fortunately, domestic varieties excel in Alaskan gardens. They make a fine, clear, rose wine.

Wash and hull strawberries and layer with sugar and crushed Campden tablet in a clean container. Cover and let stand for 48 hours. Strain juice into fermentation vessel. Add boiled water to pulp and stir; strain and add liquid to juice in fermentation bottle. (Pulp can be used in cooking later.) Add citric acid, yeast energizer, grape tannin, pectin enzyme, yeast, and cool, boiled water to top up. Insert air lock and place in a warm spot to ferment to a finish. Rack and store in a cool, dark place until clear. Rack again and bottle.

RAPID REFERENCE SECTION

Steps in Making Wine

1. Gather plant material.

2. Wash and hull plant material.

3. Extract juice by adding sugar and/or water.

4. Cover and let stand for prescribed period.

5. Strain juice into fermenting jar.

6. Add remainder of ingredients.

7. Top up with cool, boiled water, if necessary.

8. Insert air lock.

9. Place in a warm spot to ferment.

10. Siphon wine from lees into storage jars.

11. Taste.

12. Insert sterile cotton ball into mouth of bottles and close, but not tightly, so venting can occur.

13. Store in cool, dark place until clear.

14. Siphon wine into final storage bottles.

15. Taste, and blend if desired.

16. Cork.

17. Seal.

18. Store bottles on sides in cool, dark place.

Equipment Checklist

For one gallon of wine:

one-gallon jar or plastic container with cover

glass or plastic measuring cup

wooden stirring spoon

plastic colander or sieve

plastic funnel

cheesecloth or jelly bag

kitchen scale

bottle brush

one-gallon or four-liter fermentation bottle

air lock

plastic siphon hose

one-gallon or four-liter, or two half-gallon, storage bottle(s) with lid(s)

sterile cotton balls

wine bottles for final storage

new, or used but intact, corks

heavy paper

string

For five gallon batches:

glass or plastic measuring cup

large, good-quality plastic bags

six-gallon plastic garbage pail, or 10-gallon plastic food container, with lid

wooden stirring spoon

plastic colander or sieve

plastic funnel

cheesecloth or jelly bag

kitchen scale

bottle brush

five-gallon glass, or food-quality plastic, fermentation jar

air lock

plastic siphon hose

four four-liter, or five one-gallon, storage bottles, with lids

sterile cotton balls

wine bottles for final storage

new, or used but intact, corks

heavy paper

string

WINE MAKING SUPPLIERS

Alaska Mill and Feed, 1501 E. 1st Ave., Anchorage, Alaska

The Wagon Wheel, 1506 Ocean Dr., Homer, Alaska

The Compleat Winemaker, 1219 Main St., St. Helena, Calif. 94574

California Glass Co., 131025 S. Warnock Rd., Oregon City, Ore.

Wine-Art Oregon, 2758 NE Broadway, Portland, Ore.

Brewers Warehouse, 4520 Union Bay Pl. NE, Seattle, Wash.

Liberty Malt Supply Co., 1418 Western, Seattle, Wash.

Milan Home Wine and Beers, 57 Spring, NY, NY 10012-4199

OTHER BOOKS ON WINE MAKING

Amateur Winemaking, S.M. Tritton

The Art of Making Wine, Stanley F. Anderson

Beer and Wine Making Illustrated Dictionary, Leo Zanelli

Bull Cook and Authentic Historical Recipes and Practices, George Leonard Herter

Drink Your Own Garden, Judith Glover

Guidelines to Practical Winemaking, Julius Fessler

Home Made Country Wines, Dorothy Wise

Home Wines of North America, Dorothy Alatorre

Making Wine, Beer and Merry, Kathleen Howard and Norman Gibat

Tritton's Guide to Better Wine and Beer Making for Beginners, S.M. Tritton

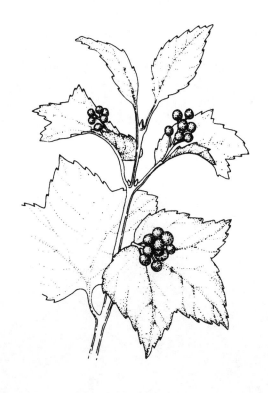

INDEX

air locks,   15, 17, 25
blending,   18, 28
Campden tablets,   13, 18, 32
clarifying,   18
corking,   28-30
dextrose,   18
equipment,   15-16, 56-57
fermentation,   12, 13, 15, 16, 17, 18, 25-27, 31
fining,   18, 32
flatness,   32
flowers of wine,   19, 32
grape tannin,13, 19, 32
haze,   31
hydrometer,16, 19
mustiness,   31
pectin enzyme,   13, 19
potassium metabisulfite,   13, 19
racking,   19, 26-28
ropiness,   32
sodium metabisulfite,   13, 19
sterlizing,   19
sugar,11, 12
sulfites,   13
topping up,   20, 25, 27
venting,   21, 28
yeast,   11, 12, 21, 25
yeast energizer,   12, 21, 31
yeast nutrient,   12, 21

OTHER BOOKS FROM WIZARD WORKS

Alaska Dictionary and Pronunciation Guide
155 pages of fact and fancy about Alaska.
Contains more than 400 definitions and nearly 50 cartoons.
Find out what Alaskans mean when they say the things they do.
ISBN 0-9621543-0-X
$8.50

Flights of Fancy
Alaska birds in verse.
Light poems about nearly two dozen common Alaska birds.
Beautifully illustrated by one of Alaska's foremost ornithologists.
ISBN 0-9621543-4-2
$7.95

Kids' Guide to Common Alaska Critters
32 fact-filled pages about a variety of Alaska wildlife .
Characteristics of more than 40 animals, from bats to wolves.
Beautiful, full-color illustrations.
Vocabulary builder.
ISBN 0-9621543-3-4
$7.95

Mt. Augustine
The 1986 eruption in 20 pages of information and photographs.
Chronology of the event, history of the mountain and
original commentary in verse.
$3.50

Alaska Small Press Catalog
Listing of selected books about Alaska by Alaskans.
Categories include Alaska Native, children's books, cooking,
history, nature and travel.
$1

To order any of these books or additional copies of this book, please send a check for the price of the book or books plus $1.50 postage and handling for the first book and $.50 for each additional book to:

Wizard Works
P.O. Box 1125
Homer, AK 99603

Order Blank

Please send me:

____	**Alaska Backyard Wines**	$____
____	**Alaska Dictionary**	$____
____	**Flights of Fancy**	$____
____	**Kids' Guide to Common Alaska Critters**	$____
____	**Alaska Small Press Catalog**	$____
Postage		$____
Total Enclosed		$____

Name_____

Address_____

City/State_____**Zip**_____